C000145326

REPTILES ROCK!

INVESTIGATE!

IGUANAS
HAVE AN EXTRA EYE!

BY ELISE TOBLER

Enslow
PUBLISHING

Please visit our website, www.enslow.com. For a free color catalog of all our high-quality books, call toll free 1-800-398-2504 or fax 1-877-980-4454.

Library of Congress Cataloging-in-Publication Data

Names: Tobler, Elise, 1970– author.
Title: Iguanas have an extra eye! / Elise Tobler.
Description: New York : Enslow Publishing, [2021] | Series: Reptiles rock!
  | Includes index.
Identifiers: LCCN 2019050708 | ISBN 9781978518261 (library binding) | ISBN
  9781978518247 (paperback) | ISBN 9781978518254 (6 Pack) | ISBN 9781978518278
  (ebook)
Subjects: LCSH: Iguanas—Juvenile literature.
Classification: LCC QL666.L25 T63 2021 | DDC 597.95/42dc23
LC record available at https://lccn.loc.gov/2019050708

Published in 2021 by
Enslow Publishing
101 West 23rd Street, Suite #240
New York, NY 10011

Copyright © 2021 Enslow Publishing

Designer: Laura Bowen
Editor: Elise Tobler

Photo credits: Cover, p. 1 (iguana) Dicky Asmoro/Shutterstock.com; cover, p. 1–32 (leaves border) Marina Solva/Shutterstock.com; p. 4 hsvrs/iStock/Getty Images Plus/Getty Images; p. 5 (iguana) Flavio Vallenari/E+/Getty Images; p. 5 (map) Peter Hermes Furian/Shutterstock.com; p. 7 benedek/iStock/Getty Images Plus/Getty Images; p. 9 Photostock-Israel/Science Photo Library/Science Photo Library/Getty Images; p. 10 Amar Grover/AWL Images/Getty Images Plus/Getty Images; p. 11 Albert photo/Moment/Getty Images Plus/Getty Images; p. 13 asbe/E+/Getty Images; p. 15 USO/iStock/Getty Images Plus/Getty Images; p. 17 Kommuguri Udaya Bhaskar/EyeEm/EyeEm/Getty Images; p. 19 Juergen Ritterbach/DigitalVision/Getty Images; p. 21 Reinhard Dirscherl/WaterFrame/Getty Images Plus Getty Images; p. 22 piccaya/iStock/Getty Images Plus/Getty Images; p. 23 Geraint Rowland Photography/Moment/Getty Images; p. 24 Wild Horizon/Contributor/ Universal Images Group Editorial/Getty Images; p. 25 De Agostini Picture Library/Contributor/De Agostini Editorial/Getty Images; p. 26 NurPhoto/Contributor/NurPhoto/Getty Images; p. 27 luchik08/Shutterstock.com; p. 29 skibreck/iStock/Getty Images Plus/Getty Images.

Portions of this work were originally authored by Kathleen Connors and published as *Iguanas*. All new material this edition authored by Elise Tobler.

All rights reserved. No part of this book may be reproduced in any form without permission in writing from the publisher, except by a reviewer.

Printed in the United States of America

Some of the images in this book illustrate individuals who are models. The depictions do not imply actual situations or events.

CPSIA compliance information: Batch #BS20ENS: For further information contact Enslow Publishing, New York, New York, at 1-800-398-2504.

Find us on

CONTENTS

Words in the glossary appear in **bold** type the first time they are used in the text.

NICE TO MEET YOU

green iguana

There are 35 species, or kinds, of iguana throughout the world, but the green iguana is the most common. Iguanas come in many shapes and colors, but they all have a spiky dorsal crest!

Adult iguanas are anywhere from 5 to 6 feet (1.5 to 1.8 m) in length, including their tail. Males tend to be larger than females, weighing up to 8 pounds (3.6 kg). Some green iguanas were found to weigh as much as 20 pounds (9 kg) and measure 6.6 feet (2 m) long!

THE GREEN IGUANA'S RANGE

CENTRAL AMERICA

SOUTH AMERICA

Iguanas like to live where it's warm, like most reptiles.

green iguana range

blue iguana

GET THE FACTS!

More than half of an iguana's length is because of its tail. If an iguana is kept as a pet, the size of its cage does not affect the size it will grow to.

5

BIG AND COLORFUL

Iguanas come in many colors, from gray to blue to bright green. In 1986, pink iguanas were found in the Galápagos Islands. These pink iguanas are considered critically endangered, meaning there aren't many of them left in the wild.

The blue iguana is one of the few naturally colored blue animals in the world. Blue iguanas used to live in great numbers on Grand Cayman Island, but **habitat** loss and **predation** by dogs have greatly reduced their population.

6

Many of the iguanas in the Galápagos Islands are **endangered!**

GET THE FACTS!

Iguanas only change color under certain conditions. Stress can make an iguana turn dark green or black!

SPINES AND SCALES

Take a close look at an iguana, and you will see how different its skin is! Like many other reptiles, iguanas are covered in rough skin called **scales**. This skin makes it hard for predators to bite iguanas. It also allows iguanas to take in sunlight, which helps keep them warm.

See the big, round scale beneath the iguana's eye? That's called a "subtympanic shield," and it sits beneath the iguana's ear hole. This shield doesn't do anything fancy, but it may fool predators into thinking it's another eye watching them.

subtympanic
shield

Iguanas are built
to stay safe. Their
skin is like armor.

GET THE FACTS!

Iguanas have a ridge of skin called
a **dewlap** on their chin.

9

THE EYES
HAVE IT

Iguanas have a third "eye" on the top of their head! It can only detect changes in light and dark. It does not see like a regular eye does. But it can help iguanas avoid predators because it allows them to sense birds flying overhead.

third eye

This body part is called a parietal eye, and it's attached to the walls of iguanas' scales. Some reptiles, salamanders, frogs, certain bony fish, sharks, and eels have these. Other reptiles like turtles and crocodiles do not have this third eye.

The parietal eye is the pale scale on top of the iguana's head.

GET THE FACTS!

The parietal eye is photoreceptive, which means it can tell when light changes. When a bird flies between the iguana and the sun, the light flickers. This tells the iguana something is up there, and it knows to hide.

11

TAIL ME MORE

When an iguana is under attack from a predator, its tail can be used like a whip to strike the predator and allow the iguana to escape. Given the length of an iguana's tail (sometimes longer than its whole body!), this whip can be painful to predators.

GET THE FACTS!

When a lizard "drops" its tail, the tail can grow back, but it will often be a different color than the body, since it's new.

Like those of some other reptiles, an iguana's tail can fall off. This can be helpful when they are trying to escape from predators. It also helps them to avoid being caught in doors or on tree branches. When the tail comes off, it doesn't hurt the iguana. And, in fact, they can regrow their tails!

Look how long the iguana's tail is compared to its body!

LUNCHTIME!

Iguanas are herbivores. That means they eat plants and fruits but not meat. Unlike other reptiles, iguanas don't eat bugs. They like tree leaves, flowers, and even cactus. Their mouth and teeth are specially **adapted** to eating fruits and vegetables.

If you're keeping an iguana as a pet, be sure to check with the pet store to see what kind of food it likes best. Never feed iguanas crickets or worms, as this won't be what they like. But giving them too many plants can also be bad for them.

This iguana is eating a prickly pear cactus!

GET THE FACTS!

Sometimes, iguanas will eat small insects and eggs and other non-plant matter, even though this isn't thought to be good for them. You should never feed them avocados because they are toxic to iguanas!

WHERE IN THE WORLD?

Iguana habitats are found in all of the Americas. Two kinds of iguana live on the Galápagos Islands, and three different species are found in Fiji. The Madagascar iguana lives on the island it's named for, which is off the southeastern coast of Africa.

Depending on the kind of iguana, it may spend more time in trees than on the ground. Some, like the green iguana, make their home in the rain forest. Other kinds of iguana prefer to live in the desert heat of places like Nevada, Utah, and Arizona.

Iguanas may be seen on the ground but also in trees!

GET THE FACTS!

Iguanas like warm places because their bodies have no way of making heat on their own. They like tropical places, beaches, deserts, and wet rain forests. The sunshine helps warm their blood and keep them active.

17

COLD-BLOODED

Most of the time, iguanas may look like they're just lying around. Like other reptiles, iguanas are cold-blooded. This means their body temperature depends on their surroundings. If they are in a cool forest, they are cooler. If they are in a desert, or the direct sun, they are warmer.

Air temperature can affect an iguana's color. When they're cold, iguanas may become slightly darker in color to take in more heat from the sun. If the temperature is too warm, these lizards might become lighter in color.

Iguanas often rest on rocks, which are warmed by the sun.

GET THE FACTS!

Sometimes, the air gets so chilled, even in warm places, that iguanas can freeze. In 2018, a cold snap in Florida had iguanas falling out of trees. As the sunshine warmed their bodies and blood, they woke up and were active again.

SEA IGUANAS

Scientist Charles Darwin first saw iguanas in the Galápagos Islands. He said they were ugly and clumsy and thought they were disgusting. The iguanas he saw were marine iguanas, and they helped Darwin come up with his **theories** of **evolution**.

Marine iguanas are good swimmers. They can stay underwater for an hour, but they usually spend only 5 to 10 minutes underwater. They often have a white "wig," from sneezing sea salt onto their heads.

GET THE FACTS!

The marine iguanas in the Galapagos Islands are often dark in color, which helps them absorb more sunlight and keep warm. During some seasons, they may be brighter colors because of all the seaweed they eat.

A marine iguana can dive as deep as 80 feet (24 m)!

FAMILY MATTERS

When it comes time to find a **mate**, male iguanas may fight each other to prove who is stronger. They may look like they're dancing a little bit. They move around in an attempt to get a female iguana's attention. Head-bobbing and patrolling their territory are common.

This female iguana is guarding her nest of eggs.

Some iguanas change color when mating time comes. Both males and females may turn an orange-red color, though males commonly become a brighter orange-red. This can happen all over their body or just on their dewlap, crest, spines, or legs.

GET THE FACTS!

Iguanas are more social than some other lizards. Female iguanas may travel up to 1.8 miles (3 km) to reach their nesting grounds, where they compete with other females for the best place to build a nest.

23

LITTLE LIZARDS

About two months after mating, female iguanas lay eggs. They can lay as many as 40 or 50 eggs at one time. That's a lot of iguana babies! A group of eggs is called a clutch, and clutches are buried in nests commonly dug in sandy soil.

iguana nest

GET THE FACTS!

Iguanas lay so many eggs because not all of them will hatch. Some don't grow properly, while others may be eaten by predators. Iguana eggs usually hatch in the spring. Sometimes, humans will eat iguana eggs the way they do chicken eggs.

It takes about three to four months for the babies to hatch, or come out of their eggs. It may take as long as a week for them to be out of their egg fully. Baby iguanas use their claws to help them get out. Baby iguanas are called hatchlings.

These rhinoceros iguanas are hatching from their eggs!

IGUANAS AS PETS

Iguanas are one of the reptiles you can keep as a pet. They grow to be pretty big, so you'll need enough space to keep one. You should also be sure you can find a **veterinarian** who treats iguanas because your pet will need a checkup!

The cage or habitat you keep the iguana in will also need a heating lamp because iguanas can't keep warm on their own. This light will be like the sun, and it will help keep your iguana warm and happy.

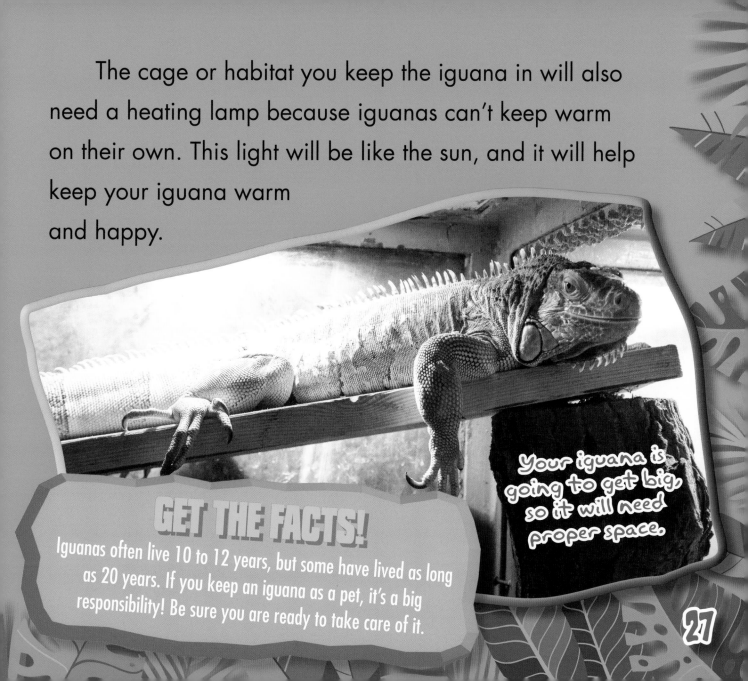

Your iguana is going to get big, so it will need proper space.

GET THE FACTS!

Iguanas often live 10 to 12 years, but some have lived as long as 20 years. If you keep an iguana as a pet, it's a big responsibility! Be sure you are ready to take care of it.

FUTURE IGUANAS

Like many wild animals, iguanas are losing their natural habitats to humans. When people build houses and roads, trees that shelter iguanas are cut down. Dogs and other animals have also been brought into iguana habitats, and often they will find and eat iguana eggs.

If we care for our world and the rain forests, we can also help care for wild iguanas. Many zoos also have **breeding** programs for iguanas. The San Diego Zoo is one place that has a good number of endangered iguanas.

If we take care of
Earth, we'll help
save the iguanas.

GET THE FACTS!

On the Galápagos Islands, the Galápagos pink land iguana is critically endangered. When scientists last counted, they found only 192 of them living in the wild.

GLOSSARY

adapt To change to suit conditions.

breeding Having to do with taking care of animals in order to produce more animals of a particular kind.

dewlap A fold of loose skin hanging from the neck or throat of an animal.

endangered In danger of dying out.

evolution The process of animals and plants slowly changing into new forms over thousands of years.

habitat The place or type of place where a plant or animal naturally or normally lives or grows.

mate One of two animals that come together to make babies. Also, to come together to make babies.

predation The act of preying on other animals.

scale One of many small, thin plates covering the bodies of some animals.

theory An explanation based on facts that is generally accepted by scientists.

veterinarian A doctor who is trained to treat animals.

FOR MORE INFORMATION

Books

Bodden, Valerie. *Amazing Animals: Iguanas*. Mankato, MN: Creative Paperbacks, 2017.

Norsk, Caroline. *Iguana: Amazing Photos & Facts*. Scotts Valley, CA: CreateSpace Publishing, 2016.

Strattin, Lisa. *Facts About the Marine Iguana*. Scotts Valley, CA: CreateSpace Publishing, 2016.

Websites

Ducksters
www.ducksters.com/animals/green_iguana.php
Ducksters is a great place to begin learning about iguanas!

Live Science
www.livescience.com/51153-iguanas.html
The Live Science website contains iguana facts and pictures.

The San Diego Zoo
animals.sandiegozoo.org/animals/iguana
Check out the San Diego Zoo to learn more about iguanas.

Publisher's note to educators and parents: Our editors have carefully reviewed these websites to ensure that they are suitable for students. Many websites change frequently, however, and we cannot guarantee that a site's future contents will continue to meet our high standards of quality and educational value. Be advised that students should be closely supervised whenever they access the internet.

INDEX